MINECRAFT MATHS

GAMEPLAY
PUBLISHING

1. TRAVELING IN MINECRAFT

Matt wants to go to his friend's castle that is 100 meters away. His saddled horse travels at 10 meters per second, sprinting is 5.6 meters per second and the speed of a moving mine cart is 8 meters per second.

1) How many seconds will it take Matt to get to his friend's castle if he uses the fastest way of traveling?

   Answer:

2) How many seconds will it take Matt to get to the castle in a mine cart?

   Answer:

3) If Matt sprints for 10 seconds and then rides his horse for 2 more seconds, how far will he get?

   Answer:

2. MINECRAFT PARTY

There were 4 guests at a Minecraft party and each guest ate several slices of cake. A cake can be divided into 6 slices only.

1) If there were 4 cakes at the party and each guest ate 5 slices of cake, how many slices of cake were left over?

   Answer: ....

2) If there were only 2 cakes at the party and the guests decided to divide the cakes evenly, how many slices did each guest eat?

   Answer: ....

3) How many cakes did the guests eat, if one guest ate 9 slices of cake and other guests ate 7 slices each?

   Answer: ....

3. MULTI CROP FARM

Steve built a rectangular farm with sides measuring 20 meters by 8 meters. He is now dividing his farmland into several sections in order to grow different crops.

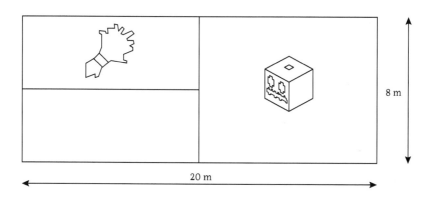

1) What is the perimeter of the farm?

   Answer: ....

2) Steve wants to plant wheat on 1/4 of the farm's area. What will be the area of the wheat plot?

   Answer: ....

3) If Steve wants the pumpkin plot to be 2 times bigger than the wheat plot, what will be the area of the pumpkin plot?

   Answer: ....

4) What fraction of the entire farm will be occupied by pumpkin?

   Answer: ....

4. SKELETON ATTACK

Steve is under skeleton attack! In order to fire back at them, he needs to craft a bow and arrows. A bow requires 3 sticks and 3 strings, while 4 arrows can be crafted from a flint, a feather and a stick.

1) How many arrows can Steve craft with 12 sticks, 12 feathers and 12 flints?

   Answer: ....

2) If 3 arrows are needed to take down 1 skeleton, how many skeletons can Steve take down with 16 arrows, assuming that he won't miss a shot?

   Answer: ....

3) Steve has 16 arrows, 4 sticks, 3 feathers and 12 flints. If he decides to craft additional arrows, how many arrows in total will he have?

   Answer: ....

5. CRAFTING AND SMELTING

Peter is preparing for a battle with the Wither. He needs to smelt iron ore in order to craft iron armor. A helmet takes 5 iron ingots to make, a chest plate takes 8, leggings take 7 and boots take 4.

— Smelting 1 block of iron ore produces 1 iron ingot
— 1 coal smelts 8 blocks of iron ore.

1) How much coal will it take to smelt enough iron ore in order to make full set of armor?

Answer:

2) If Peter wants to craft 3 iron chest plates and 2 iron boots, how much coal will he need to smelt enough iron ore for this task?

Answer:

3) Burning time of one coal is 80 seconds while burning time of one lava bucket is 920 seconds more. What is the burning time of one lava bucket?

Answer:

6. BAKING MARATHON

Steve is baking cakes for a party in the village! A cake requires 3 buckets of milk, 1 egg, 2 units of sugar and 3 units of wheat to make. Each cake has 6 slices.

1) How many cakes can Steve make with 7 buckets of milk, 2 eggs, 6 units of sugar and 8 units of wheat?

   Answer: ....

2) Steve wants to make 3 cakes but he only has 4 buckets of milk, how many more buckets of milk will he have to get?

   Answer: ....

3) If there are 13 villagers and 6 cakes, how many slices of cake can each villager get, if they all have an equal number of slices? How many slices will be left over?

   Answer: ....

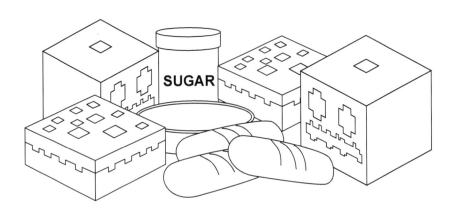

7. SURVIVAL IN THE NETHER

1) Steve will be journeying to the Nether for 60 minutes. How many 8-minute Fire Resistance potions he should bring to be protected from lava the entire time?

Answer: ....

2) If he will only be traveling in the Nether for 40 minutes, how many 3-minute Fire Resistance potions he should bring to protect himself from lava the entire time?

Answer: ....

3) If Steve will fight the Wither for 15 minutes, how many 3-minute Regeneration potions and 8-minute Strength potions does he need to make in order to have Strength and Regeneration during the entire fight?

Answer: ....

8. ARMOR STRENGTH

Dave is playing Minecraft survival game with fully armored players. Diamond armor reduces damage by 80%, whereas iron armor reduces damage by 60%. Dave's sword does 5 hearts of damage per hit.

1) Dave wants to attack a diamond-armored enemy with 10 hearts of health. How many hits will it take to destroy the enemy?

   Answer: ....

2) How many hits will it take Dave to destroy an iron-armored enemy with 10 hearts of health?

   Answer: ....

3) How many times stronger is diamond armor than iron armor?

   Answer: ....

9. MARKET DAY

1) If you take 10 emeralds to trade with a farmer villager and buy everything on the shopping list at the bottom of the page, how many emeralds will you have left?

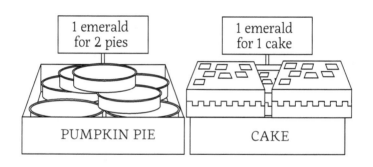

Shopping List

4 Loaves of bread   6 Cookies

10 Apples   2 Pumpkin pies

3 Cakes

Answer: ....

10. ARMOR TYPES

A helmet takes 5 units of armor material to make, a chest plate takes 8, leggings take 7 and boots take 4.

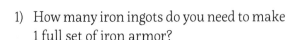

1) How many iron ingots do you need to make 1 full set of iron armor?

   Answer: ....

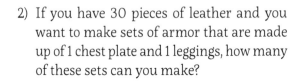

2) If you have 30 pieces of leather and you want to make sets of armor that are made up of 1 chest plate and 1 leggings, how many of these sets can you make?

   Answer: ....

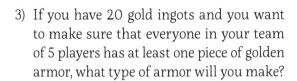

3) If you have 20 gold ingots and you want to make sure that everyone in your team of 5 players has at least one piece of golden armor, what type of armor will you make?

   Answer: ....

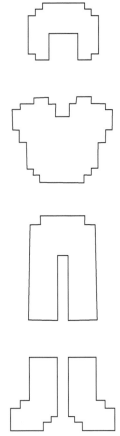

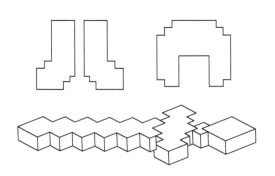

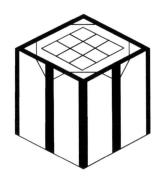

11. HEALTH REGENERATION

Steve is at 1 health point and he cannot regenerate because he is hungry! He doesn't have normal food, so he has to either eat a golden apple or brew up a potion. Full health bar is 20 health points.

1) A golden apple provides 5 seconds of Regeneration II. If the effect gives Steve one health point every 1.25 seconds, how many golden apples does he need to eat if he wants to fully restore his health bar?

Answer: ....

2) Healing I potion restores 4 health points. Each glistering melon can make 3 Healing I potions. How many glistering melons does Steve need if he plans on consuming only Healing I potions to heal himself to full health?

Answer: ....

3) How many Healing I potions does he need to use to fully restore his health?

Answer: ....

12. VOLUME AND SURFACE AREA

Kate is using ice blocks to build an igloo, a type of snow hut. Each side of an ice block is 1 meter.

1) Find the combined volume of these ice blocks?

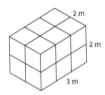

Answer: _____

2) Find the surface area of this block which is made up of several ice blocks?

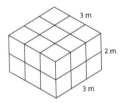

Answer: _____

3) What is the combined volume of these ice blocks?

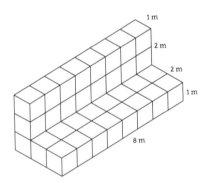

Answer: _____

13. TREASURE CHEST

Steve has been investigating an abandoned mineshaft. He found a chest with 57 units of different ores.

— He has 12 lumps of coal and 3 gold ingots
— He has 4 less diamonds than coal
— He has twice as much lapis lazuli as diamonds
— The number of iron ingots is equal to the number of coal lumps and gold ingots added together. The rest is redstone.

How much of each item did he find?

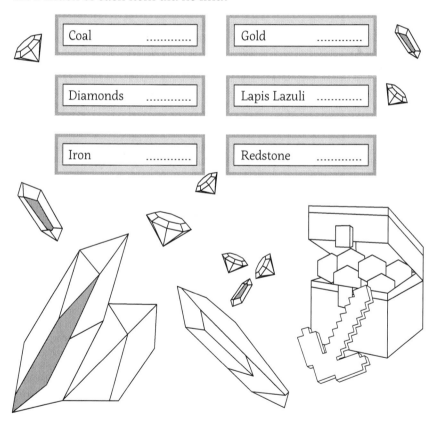

| Coal | .... |

| Gold | .... |

| Diamonds | .... |

| Lapis Lazuli | .... |

| Iron | .... |

| Redstone | .... |

14. CAVE SPIDER ATTACK

Mike stumbled upon a spider spawner in a cave and wants to use potions of Harming and Healing to fight cave spiders. Harming Potion inflicts 3 hearts of damage and Healing Potion restores 2 hearts. Cave spiders have 6 hearts of health.

1) How many Harming potions does Mike need to throw in order to destroy a cave spider with full health bar?

   Answer:

2) Mike's health bar is at 2 hearts of health because he was poisoned by a cave spider. How many Healing Potions does he need to consume to fully restore his health to 10 hearts?

   Answer:

3) If cave spiders spawn one by one, how many of them can Mike destroy with 24 potions of Harming, assuming that he won't miss a throw?

   Answer:

15. CHEST MATHS

Emma is taking stock of her food inventory which she stores in different chests. A small chests has 27 slots of inventory space and a large chest has 54 slots. Each slot can fit a stack of items.

— Eggs stack up to a maximum of 16
— Cookies stack up to a maximum of 64
— Cakes, rabbit stews and mushroom stews are not stackable

1) Emma plans to fill up 2 large chests and 3 small chests with cookies. What is the maximum number of cookies can she fit into the chests?

   Answer: ....

2) Emma placed 5 full stacks of eggs, 3 full stacks of cookies, 10 cakes, 1 rabbit stew and 1 mushroom stew in a small chest. How many units of food items does Emma have in this chest?

   Answer: ....

3) What is the maximum amount of eggs can Emma store in a large chest?

   Answer: ....

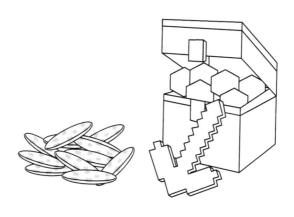

16. COMBAT

Harry is ready for combat and is fully equipped with diamond armor and a sword! His diamond sword can inflict 3.5 hearts of damage per hit.

1) If Harry will fight a wounded creeper that has only 7 hearts of health left, how many strikes will it take to bring the creeper down?

   Answer: ....

2) Harry is surrounded by 3 zombies with 10 hearts of health each. How many strikes will it take to bring all of them down?

   Answer: ....

3) Harry's sword damage was reduced by 1 heart during a fight with a giant spider that has 50 hearts of health. How many sword strikes will it take Harry to take down the mighty spider?

   Answer: ....

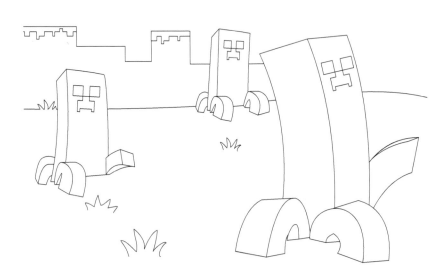

17. POTION EXPERIMENTS

1) It is 8 am. Ashton drinks an 8-minute Strength potion. One minute after the strength runs out, he drinks a 6-minute Night Vision potion. Five minutes later Ashton drinks an 8-minute Speed potion. After it runs out, he drinks a 3-minute Jumping potion. When the jumping effect wears off, what time will it be?

   Answer: ....

2) How many 3-minute Invisibility potions will Ashton have to make if he wants to stay invisible for 24 minutes?

   Answer: ....

3) Will he need to make one more to stay invisible for 25 minutes?

   Answer: ....

18. EMERALD TRADING

Steve decided to trade with leatherworker and weapon smith villagers. The leatherworker buys 9 units of leather for 1 emerald and sells saddles for 8 emeralds each. The weapon smith buys 3 diamonds for 1 emerald.

1) If Steve sold 18 units of leather to the leatherworker and 6 diamonds to the weapon smith, how many emeralds did he receive?

   Answer: ....

2) Steve wants to buy 3 saddles. How many emeralds will he have to spend?

   Answer: ....

3) How many emeralds will Steve receive if he sells 24 diamonds to the weapon smith?

   Answer: ....

19. WHEAT FARM

Robert is preparing bread for breakfast. To craft a loaf of bread he needs 3 units of wheat. One unit of wheat grows on one block of farmland.

1) Robert has a rectangular wheat farm with 5 blocks width and 6 blocks length. If all wheat on the farm has already matured, how many loaves of bread can Robert make?

   Answer: ....

2) If only 40% of the wheat on Robert's farm has fully matured, how many loaves of bread can he make?

   Answer: ....

3) There are 8 people in Robert's family (including himself). At least how big should Robert's wheat farm be to feed each family member 1 bread loaf every day if only half of the wheat on the farm matures every day?

   Answer: ....

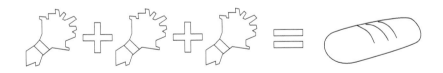

20. MOB REPELLENT HOME

Steve knows that mobs don't spawn on glass, so he decided to use glass blocks to pave some areas within his living compounds. Each side of a glass block and a glass pane is 1 meter.

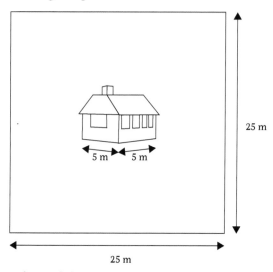

1) If the area of Steve's house is two times less than 50 square meters, how many glass blocks does he need to get in order to pave the entire floor of the house with glass blocks?

   Answer: ....

2) Steve's house is located in the middle of a square yard with a perimeter of 100 meters. If Steve wants to pave just the yard, how many glass blocks will he need to use?

   Answer: ....

3) To be more economical, Steve decided to pave the entire floor area inside his house with one layer of glass panes instead of glass blocks. If 6 glass blocks are required to make 16 square glass panes, at least how many glass blocks are needed for the project?

   Answer: ....

21. PARKOUR CHALLENGE

Steve with his friends Joe and Trisha decided to compete in a 30-block parkour challenge. Joe can finish the 30-block parkour course in 2 minutes, while Trisha can finish the same parkour course in 1 minute. They start the challenge at the same time.

1) If Steve can go from one block to the next in 2 seconds, how much time will it take Steve to reach the end of the parkour course, assuming he will never fall?

   Answer:

2) On what block will Trisha be when Steve will cross the finish line?

   Answer:

3) On what block will Joe be when Trisha gets to the finish line, assuming Joe can go from one block to the next in 4 seconds?

   Answer:

23

22. COW FARM

Two cows enter "love mode" when you feed them wheat and then a baby cow spawns. They will not be able to enter love mode again for 5 minutes and the baby cow starts its 20 minute journey to maturity.

1) Josh starts off with 2 cows. How many baby cows will Josh have 18 minutes after continuous breeding process?

   Answer: ....

2) The growth period of baby cows can be reduced by 10% using wheat as an accelerator. How many baby cows will Josh have 18 minutes after he begins breeding if wheat is used to speed up the journey to maturity?

   Answer: ....

3) Josh wants to craft full set of leather armor which requires 24 units of leather, but he only has 3 cows on his farm and 2 units of leather in his inventory. Each cow drops 1 unit of leather. How many additional cows does he need to breed to craft a full set of leather armor?

   Answer: ....

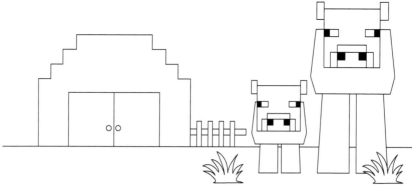

23. BUILDING A WALL

Steve is building a stone wall around his house to keep the mobs away. Each side of a stone block is 1 meter. Below is the plan of the wall:

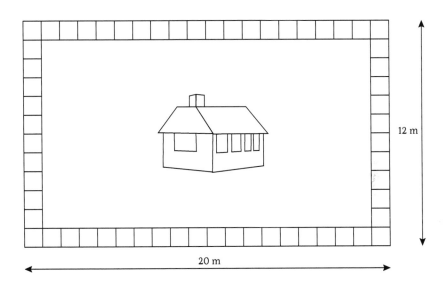

12 m

20 m

1) If the thickness of the wall is only one block, how many stone blocks will Steve need for a 5 meter-high wall?

   Answer: ....

2) An opening has been made inside the wall to create a 2 meter high and 3 meter wide entrance. How many blocks did Steve have to remove from the wall to make the entrance?

   Answer: ....

3) What will the perimeter of the wall be?

   Answer: ....

24. ADVENTURES IN THE JUNGLE

A group of 5 players discovered 4 treasure chests hidden inside a jungle temple. The first chest that was opened contained 5 diamonds.

1) How many diamonds will they find after all the chests are opened, if all four chests contain the same amount of diamonds?

   Answer: ....

2) If the group of players decide to share the diamond loot evenly between each other, how many diamonds will each one of them get?

   Answer: ....

3) It takes 4 diamonds to make diamond boots. How many boots will each player get if they use all the diamonds found in the jungle temple to craft diamond boots?

   Answer: ....

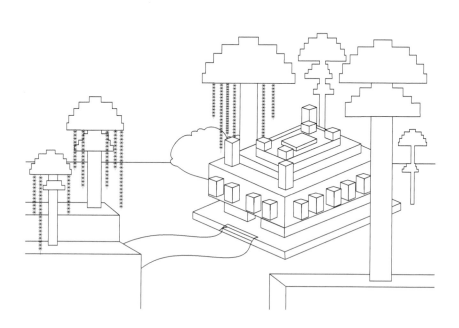

25. FUEL EFFICIENCY

Peter wants to cook his food in a furnace. He knows that different types of fuel have different efficiency:

— 1 sapling cooks 0.5 item
— 1 wood block cooks 1.5 item
— 1 blaze rod cooks 12 items

1) Peter wants to cook 5 pork chops and 2 steaks. If he only has saplings for fuel, how many saplings does he need to cook the food?

   Answer:

2) How many times more effective as a fuel is blaze rod compared to wood block?

   Answer:

3) How many wooden blocks will it take to cook 24 steaks

   Answer:

27

26. NOURISHMENT

— Maximum food level is 20 food points (🍗🍗🍗🍗🍗🍗🍗🍗🍗🍗)
— Sprinting is possible only if food level is at 6 food points (🍗🍗🍗) or above
— When the food level is at 18 points (🍗🍗🍗🍗🍗🍗🍗🍗🍗) or above, player's health will slowly regenerate

1) Steve cannot sprint as his food bar is at 2 food points only. If eating 1 carrot restores 3 food points (🍗🍗), how many carrots does he need to eat in order to be able to sprint again?

Answer: ....

2) Steve's food bar is at 1 food point and he only has steaks in his inventory. If eating 1 steak restores 8 food points (🍗🍗🍗🍗), how many steaks should he eat to begin regenerating?

Answer: ....

3) Steve's saturation level is at zero and his food bar begins to shake. If eating one bread loaf restores 6 saturation points and maximum saturation level is 20 points, how many bread loaves does Steve need to eat to fully restore his saturation?

Answer: ....

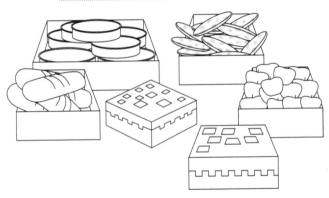

27. CHESTS, SLOTS AND STACKS

Jane is planning to store her stone and cobblestone blocks stash in various chests. A small chest has 27 slots and a large chest has double that number of slots. Both stone and cobblestone blocks stack up to a maximum of 64 units in one slot.

1) If Jane has 81 full stacks of stone blocks, how many small chests does she need to store all of the stacks?

    Answer: ....

2) How many slots in total are there in 3 large chests?

    Answer: ....

3) If Jane has 55 full stacks of stone blocks and 1 full stack of cobble-stone blocks, how many large chests does she need to store all the items?

    Answer: ....

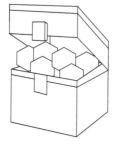 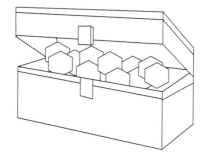

28. GRIDLOCK

Josh and Hannah are stuck in traffic. Josh looks out of his window and sees 2 creepers, 3 skeletons and 5 zombies. Hannah looks out of her window and sees 7 creepers, 8 zombies and 1 skeleton.

1) What percentage of the mobs that Josh sees are creepers?

    Answer: ....

2) What percentage of the mobs that Hannah sees are zombies?

    Answer: ....

3) What percentage of all the mobs Josh and Hannah can see are skeletons? Round the answer to the nearest whole number.

    Answer: ....

29. TRIP WIRE TRAP

Steve tripped on a tripwire that is connected to a trap! The trap is set so that it takes 3 seconds for the redstone signal to travel from the tripwire hook to the dispenser and another 2 seconds for the arrow fired from the dispenser to hit Steve. Arrows move with constant speed.

1) How many seconds will it take for the arrow to hit Steve from the moment the trap is triggered?

   Answer: ....

2) If the dispenser fires 10 arrows one after another, how many arrows will Steve get 8 seconds from the moment he tripped on the tripwire?

   Answer: ....

3) Arrows fired from dispensers do 3 health points (♡◗) of damage. If Steve's health bar is at 20 health points, how many arrow hits will it take to kill Steve?

   Answer: ....

4) How many seconds will it take for the arrow to hit Steve from the moment he triggered the trap if he steps back and doubles the distance between him and the dispenser?

   Answer: ....

30. DAY-NIGHT CYCLE

The day-night cycle in Minecraft is a 20 minute long lapse between two main light settings. A day is 10 minutes long. Sunset and dawn are 1.5 minutes each.

1) How long is a night in Minecraft?

   Answer: ....

2) If you went to bed just as the sunset stage began and woke up right at the end of the night, how many minutes did you sleep?

   Answer: ....

3) Chris has been exploring the jungle for the whole day and saw ocelots every 30 seconds throughout the day. How many ocelots did Chris see that day?

   Answer: ....

SOLUTIONS

1. TRAVELING IN MINECRAFT
1) 10 seconds = 100 m ÷ 10 m/s
2) 12.5 seconds = 100 m ÷ 8 m/s
3) 76 meters = 10 s × 5.6 m/s + 2 s × 10 m/s

2. MINECRAFT PARTY
1) 4 slices = 4 cakes × 6 slices - 4 guests × 5 slices
2) 3 slices each = 2 cakes × 6 slices ÷ 4 guests
3) 5 cakes = (9 slices × 1 guest + 7 slices × 3 guests) ÷ 6

3. MULTI CROP FARM
1) 56 meters = 20 m × 2 + 8 m × 2
2) 40 m^2 = x (20m × 8m)
3) 80 m^2 = 40 m2 × 2
4) 1/2 = 80 m2 ÷ 160 m2

4. SKELETON ATTACK
1) 48 arrows = 12 × 4 arrows
2) at most 5 skeletons; 16 arrows ÷ 3 arrows
3) 28 arrows = 16 arrows + 3 feathers × 4 arrows

5. CRAFTING AND SMELTING
1) 3 coal = 24 iron ingots ÷ 8
2) 4 coal = (3×8 iron ingots + 2×4 iron ingots) ÷ 8
3) 1000 seconds = 80 sec + 920 sec

6. BAKING MARATHON
1) only 2 cakes can be made if 2 eggs are available
2) 5 buckets of milk = 3 buckets of milk × 3-4 buckets of milk
3) 2 slices each = (6 cakes × 6 slices) ÷ 13 villagers, 10 slices left over = 6 cakes × 6 slices - 2 slices × 13 villagers

7. SURVIVAL IN THE NETHER
1) 8 potions; 60 min ÷ 8 min
2) 14 potions; 40 min ÷ 3 min
3) 5 Regeneration potions = 15 min ÷ 3 min
   2 Strength potions; 15 min ÷ 8 min

8. ARMOR STRENGTH
1) 10 hits; 5 hearts × 0.2 = 1 heart of damage per hit, 10 hearts ÷ 1 = 10 hits
2) 5 hits; 5 × 0.4 = 2 hearts of damage per hit; 10 ÷ 2 = 5 hits
3) 2 times stronger; 10 hits ÷ 5 hits = 2

9. MARKET DAY
1) 1 emerald left

10. ARMOR TYPES
1) 24 iron ingots = 5+8+7+4

2) 2 sets = 30÷(8+7)
3) boots; 20 gold ingots ÷ 5 = 4 ingots

11. HEALTH REGENERATION
1) 5 golden apples; 5 ÷ 1.25 = 4 health points per golden apple, 1 health point + 5 golden apples × 4 health points > 20 health points
2) 2 glistering melons; 3×4 = 12 health points per 1 glistering melon, 1 health point + 2 glistering melons × 12 > 20 health points
3) 5 Healing I potions; 1 health point + 5 Healing I × 4 health points > 20 health points

12. VOLUME AND SURFACE AREA
1) 12 m^3 = 2 m × 2 m × 3 m
2) 42 m^2 = 2 m × 3 m × 4 + 3 m × 3 m × 2
3) 40 m^3 = 1 m × 8 m × 3 m + 1 m × 8 m × 2 m

13. TREASURE CHEST
12 coal lumps, 3 gold ingots, 8 diamonds, 16 lapis lazuli, 15 iron ingots, 3 redstones

14. CAVE SPIDER ATTACK
1) 2 Harming potions = 6 hearts ÷ 3
2) 4 Healing potions; 2 hearts + 4 Healing potions × 2 hearts = 10 hearts
3) 12 cave spiders = 24 potions × 3 hearts of damage ÷ 6 hearts

15. CHEST MATHS
1) 12096 units = 64×(2 large chests × 54 slots + 3 small chests × 27 slots)
2) 284 food items = 80 eggs + 192 cookies + 10 cakes + 1 rabbit stew + 1 mushroom stew
3) 864 eggs = 54 slots x 16

16. COMBAT
1) 2 strikes = 7 hearts ÷ 3.5 hearts of damage
2) 9 strikes = 3 zombies × 10 hearts ÷ 3.5 hearts of damage
3) 20 strikes; 3.5 - 1 = 2.5 hearts of damage per strike, 50 ÷ 2.5 = 20 strikes

17. POTION EXPERIMENTS
1) 8:25am
2) 8 Invisibility potions = 24 min ÷ 3 min
3) yes

18. EMERALD TRADING
1) 4 emeralds = 2+2
2) 24 emeralds = 3×8
3) 8 emeralds = 24÷3

19. WHEAT FARM
1) 10 bread loaves; $5 \times 6 = 30$ wheat matured, 30 wheat $\div 3 = 10$ bread
2) 4 bread loaves; $0.4 \times 30 = 12$ wheat matured, 12 wheat $\div 3 = 4$ bread
3) 48 wheat = 8 people $\times 3$ wheat $\times 2$

20. MOB REPELLENT HOME
1) 25 glass blocks = $50 \text{ m}^2 \div 2$
2) 600 glass blocks = $25 \text{ m} \times 25 \text{ m} - 25 \text{ m}^2$
3) 10 glass blocks; $6 \times 25 \div 16 = 9.3$, i.e. at least 10 glass blocks

21. PARKOUR CHALLENGE
1) 1 minute = $2 \times 30 = 60$ seconds
2) 30th block or finish line (it's a tie)
3) 15th block = 60 seconds $\div 4$

22. COW FARM
1) 4 baby cows
2) 3 baby cows
3) 19 cows = 24-3-2

23. BUILDING A WALL
1) 300 stone blocks = $20\text{m} \times 5\text{m} \times 2 + 10\text{m} \times 5 \text{ m} \times 2$
2) 6 stone blocks = $2 \text{ m} \times 3 \text{ m}$
3) 64 meters = $20 \text{ m} \times 2 + 12 \text{ m} \times 2$

24. ADVENTURES IN THE JUNGLE
1) 20 diamonds = 4 chests $\times 5$ diamonds
2) 4 diamonds each = 20 diamonds $\div 5$ players
3) 1 pair of boots each; 20 diamonds $\div 4$ diamonds = 5 pairs of boots

25. FUEL EFFICIENCY
1) 14 saplings = 7 items $\div 0.5$
2) 8 times more effective = $12 \div 1.5$
3) 16 wooden blocks = 24 items $\div 1.5$

26. NOIRISHMENT
1) 2 carrots; 2 food points + 3 food points $\times 2$ carrots > 6 food points
2) 3 steaks; 1 food point + 8 food points $\times 3$ steaks > 18 food points
3) 4 bread loaves

27. CHESTS, SLOTS AND STACKS
1) 3 small chests = 81 stacks $\div 27$ slots
2) 162 slots = 27 slots $\times 2 \times 3$
3) 2 large chests

28. GRIDLOCK
1) 20% = 2 creepers $\div 10$ mobs
2) 50% = 8 zombies $\div 16$ mobs
3) 15% = 4 skeletons $\div 26$ mobs

29. TRIP WIRE TRAP
1) 5 seconds = 2 seconds + 3 seconds
2) 2 arrows; 5 seconds for 1st arrow and 2 seconds for 2nd arrow
3) 7 arrow hits; 3 health points $\times 7$ arrow hits > 20 health points
4) 7 seconds = 3 seconds + 2 seconds $\times 2$

30. DAY-NIGHT CYCLE
1) 7 minutes = 20 min – 10 min – (1.5 min $\times 2$)
2) 8.5 minutes = 1.5 min + 7 min
3) 20 ocelots = 10 min $\times 60$ sec $\div 30$ sec

13677513R00021

Printed in Great Britain
by Amazon.co.uk, Ltd.,
Marston Gate.